First published in 2026 by

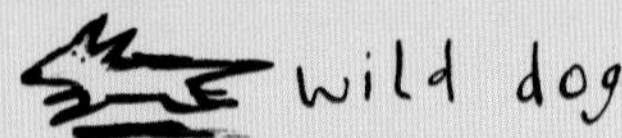

Melbourne, Australia
wdog.com.au



ISBN: 978-1-74203-707-3

10 9 8 7 6 5 4 3 2 1    26 27 28 29 30

Printed and bound in China by Everbest Printing Investment Limited

Wild Dog would like to thank Dr T. Franciscus Scheelings for his careful fact checking.

A catalogue record for this book is available from the National Library of Australia

FSC® is a non-profit international organisation established to promote the responsible management of the world's forests.

Image Credits: front cover finchfocus; pp2–3 Michiel de Wit; p5 Johan Swanepoel; pp6–7 Nine_Tomorrows; pp8–9 Anton Shahrai; p8 (inset, left) slowmotiongli; p8 (inset, right) Ocimadfoto; p9 (inset, left) Martin Pelanek; p9 (inset, centre) Milan Zygmunt; p9 (inset, right) Uwe Bergwitz; pp10–11 Cavan-Images; p11 (inset, left) Tanguy de Saint-Cyr; p11 (inset, right) Vladislav T. Jirousek; pp12–13 DINAL_SAMARASINGHE; p13 (inset) Ery Azmeer; pp14–15 Brooke Ottley; p15 (inset) Alessio Rinaldi; pp16–17 Christopher Robin Smith Photography; p16 (inset, top) lisdiyanto suhardjo; p16 (inset, bottom) Tyrrannoid; p17 (inset, top) Uwe Bergwitz; p17 (inset, bottom) PeterVrabel; pp18–19 Calek; p18 (inset) Supermop; pp20–21 EcoPrint; p21 (inset) GUDKOV ANDREY; pp22–23 Janelle Lugge; pp24–25 Uckarintra Wongcharit; pp26–27 Somluck Rungaree; pp28–29 finchfocus; pp30–31 Michiel de Wit; back cover Supermop.

UP CLOSE

wild dog

LISA McLELLAN

# CROCODILES

Crocodiles have existed for more than 200 million years. That means they shared the earth with dinosaurs! Crocodiles belong to a group of ancient reptiles called crocodilians. There are 28 living **SPECIES** of crocodilians. Many extinct species were much bigger or smaller than today's crocodiles.

There were crocodilians that ate plants rather than meat. Some had flippers rather than feet. Crocodiles are related to dinosaurs, but they **EVOLVED** independently. This means they are like cousins.

*Crocodilaemus robustus* fossil.

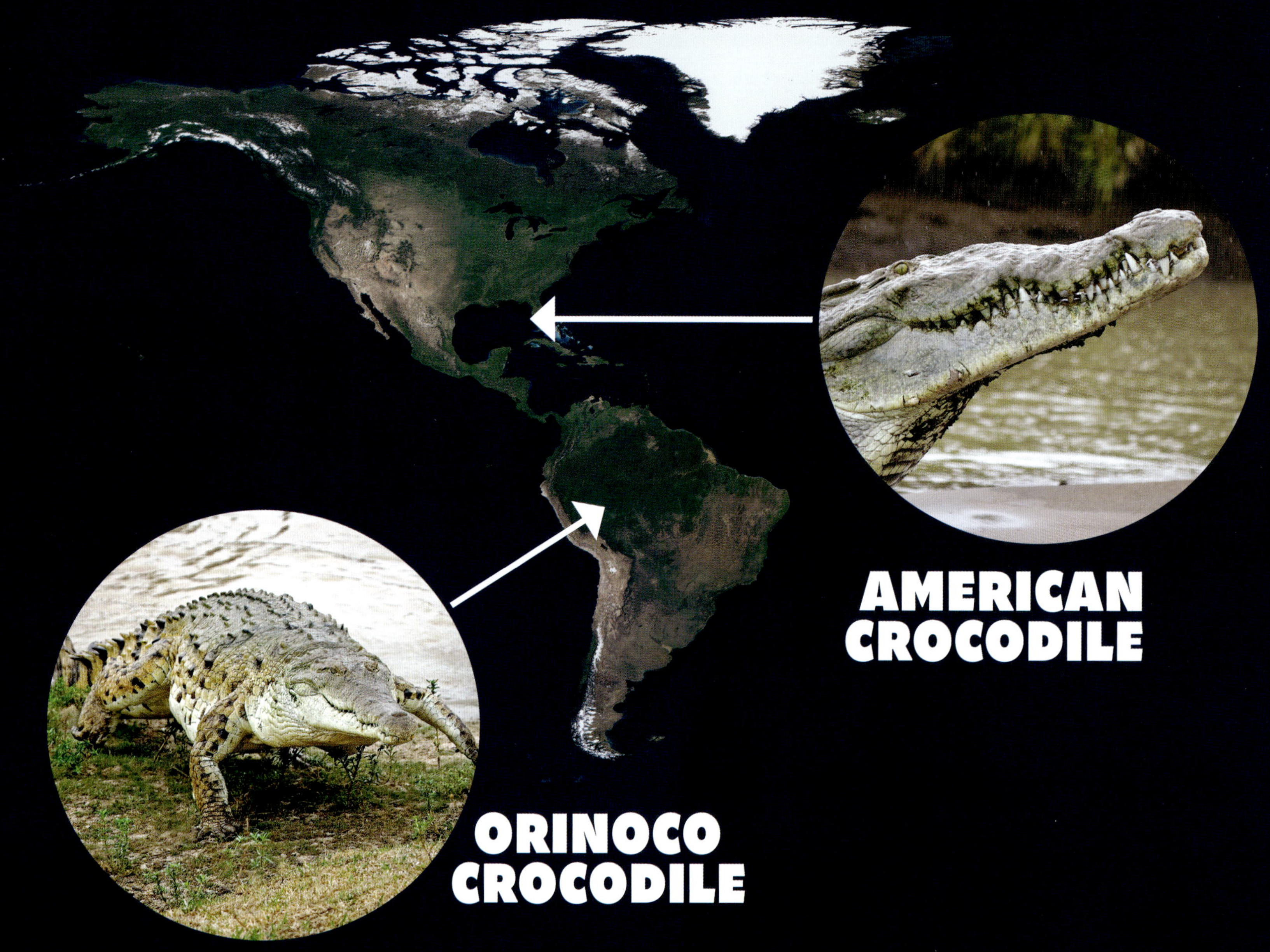


Today, crocodiles can be found on every continent except Europe and Antarctica. They are semiaquatic, so they spend time on land but live mostly in the water. You will find them in waterways in warm and **TROPICAL** climates.

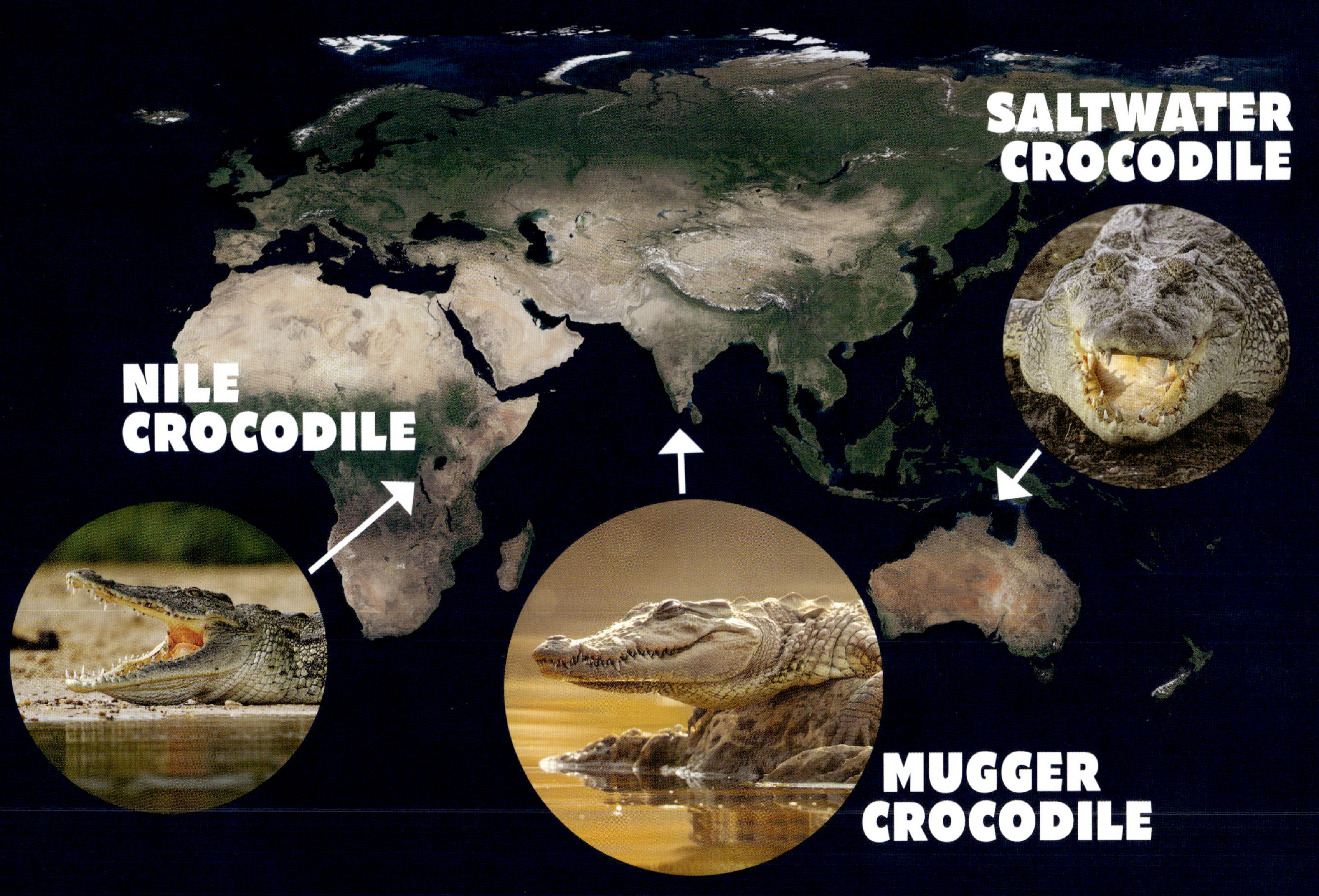


Crocodiles are members of the order **CROCODYLIA**. Tomistoma, alligators, caimans and gharials are also crocodilians. The word crocodile comes from the Greek word *krokódilos*, which means 'worm of the stones'.

Crocodilians vary in size and shape.

The saltwater crocodile is the biggest, reaching lengths of up to 6 metres. Gharials are slimmer and grow between 3 and 6 metres.

Tomistoma and alligators grow to about 4 metres. Some adult caimans are only 1 metre long.

AMERICAN ALLIGATOR

SPECTACLED CAIMAN

Crocodilians are famous for their big snapping jaws. The size and shape of their jaws differs from species to species. Saltwater crocodiles, mugger crocodiles and broad-snouted caimans all have wide snouts.

Tomistoma, gharials, Australian freshwater crocodiles and African slender-snouted crocodiles all have narrow snouts. Slim snouts are **HYDRODYNAMIC** and come in handy when a crocodilian's main food source is fish.

**INDIAN GHARIAL**

Crocodiles are **ECTOTHERMIC**. They use external sources, like the sun, to warm up or cool down. This is called thermoregulation. One reason crocodiles might need to warm up is to increase their **METABOLIC RATE**. Metabolic rate is the speed at which all bodies burn energy. Digesting a big dinner can take a lot of energy. Crocodiles often sunbake after eating to speed up their metabolic rate.

Crocodiles are covered in scales, and are sometimes mistaken for floating logs.

Crocodiles have clawed feet and webbed toes on their back feet.

Australia has the saltwater crocodile and the Australian freshwater crocodile. Both species live in the country's northern regions, from Western Australia to northern Queensland.

**SALTIES** live in rivers, estuaries, creeks, swamps, lagoons and billabongs and can tolerate water that is high in **SALINITY**.

**FRESHIES** are found further inland in freshwater lakes, rivers, estuaries and billabongs, but also sometimes in slightly salty tidal waterways.

# FRESHIES

Australian freshwater crocodiles are about 3 metres long in adulthood. They eat mostly fish, amphibians and crabs.

Freshies are shy creatures and usually bite only in self-defence. If you bump into one, it will probably swim away.

## SALTIES

Saltwater crocodiles are the biggest reptiles in the world. They grow from 3.5 to 6 metres long and weigh up to 1000 kilograms.

They eat fish and turtles, as well as larger animals such as wallabies, pigs and buffalo. Salties even eat sharks!

Some large male salties prefer to live alone. They fiercely guard their territory. Attacks on humans are rare, but you should always pay attention to warning signs in areas known for salties.

A female saltwater crocodile will build a mound for a nest. The mound is usually made from vegetation. On average, the female can lay 50 eggs at a time. Only around 1 percent of those baby crocs will reach adulthood.

The temperature of the nest determines whether the eggs will hatch as male or female. Males are produced if the temperature of the nest is 32 degrees Celsius. If the nest is much warmer or much cooler, a greater proportion of the eggs will hatch as female.

Crocodiles are around 25 to 30 centimetres long when they leave the nest. Mother crocodiles protect their babies for several months. After that, the **HATCHLINGS** are on their own. Many fall victim to freshwater turtles, birds of prey and other crocs.

Crocodiles hunt at sunrise, sunset and at night. They love to wait beneath the waterline for fish, birds and mammals. To help them hunt, crocodiles have a special third eyelid on each eye. The third eyelid is transparent and allows them to see underwater. You'll have a hard time seeing them, but they'll be able to see you!

A crocodile's diet is made up of fish, turtles, amphibians and birds. Occasionally, they will eat a large mammal, such as a cow or a buffalo.

To kill a big animal, crocodiles will first grab it in their enormous jaws and try to drown it. Then, they use their powerful tail and hind legs to perform a **DEATH ROLL**. Crocodiles cannot chew, and the death roll breaks their **PREY** into chunks small enough to swallow.

Crocodiles play an important role in the culture and lives of Australian Aboriginal people. To some groups, the crocodile is the guardian of the waterways. It encourages care for rivers and lakes. To others, the crocodile is a guide. Its appearance represents Ancestors or carries a message from them. Some groups believe that a crocodile appearing in dreams represents a hidden danger.

By observing crocodile behaviour, Aboriginal people know when it is safe to hunt, wash and swim in waterways.

**In Papua New Guinea, the Sepik region hosts an annual Crocodile Festival. The festival is both a cultural celebration and a conservation effort. It honours the bond between the Sepik people and the crocodile.**

In the past 100 years, many crocodile species have become **ENDANGERED**. This is due to hunting and habitat destruction.

Trade in their skins for fashion accessories resulted in the Australian saltwater crocodile being hunted nearly to extinction.

In Australia, crocodiles are now **PROTECTED**. The use of a sustainable conservation model also helped to rebuild populations. Today, there is thought to be around 100,000 freshwater crocodiles and up to 200,000 saltwater crocodiles.

Despite their fearsome reputation, crocodiles are an important part of the **ECOSYSTEM**. If we respect their habitat, they might exist for another 200 million years.

## CROC FACTS

- Crocodiles can live up to a year without eating.
- The bumpy, triangular scales that begin at the end of the tail and continue up a crocodile's back are called scutes.
- A crocodile running on land can reach speeds of up to 18 kilometres per hour.
- In the wild, crocodiles can live up to 70 years, but the oldest crocodile recorded in Australia lived in captivity. Mr Freshie lived to be 140 years old.
- Crocodiles communicate with vocal sounds such as grunts, squeaks and hisses. They also use visual displays, such as puffing up, snapping their jaws and slapping the water with their heads and tails.
- A saltwater crocodile can have up to 68 teeth at any time and can regrow up to 8000 teeth in its lifetime.

# GLOSSARY

**Crocodylia:** the order of reptiles known as crocodilians, which includes crocodiles, alligators, caimans, gharials and Tomistoma.

**Death roll:** when a crocodile clamps its prey in its jaws and performs a violent roll in the water to dismember its prey.

**Ecosystem:** a community of living things interacting with and dependent upon one another and their environment.

**Ectothermic:** relying on external sources to regulate metabolic rate.

**Endangered:** a species at risk of extinction.

**Evolve:** a term in biology referring to the continuous genetic adaptation of a species to their environment through factors including selection and mutation.

**Freshie:** an Australian freshwater crocodile.

**Hatchlings:** baby crocodiles.

**Hydrodynamic:** shaped for easy manoeuvring in or on water.

**Metabolic Rate:** the speed at which bodies burn energy to perform functions such as breathing, blood circulation, growth and cell production.

**Prey:** an animal hunted for food by other animals.

**Protected:** a plant or animal protected by law, meaning it can be illegal to kill or capture them.

**Salinity:** a measure of how much salt exists in a body of water.

**Saltie:** a saltwater crocodile.

**Species:** a population of living things capable of reproducing.

**Tropical:** regions with periods of high humidity and pronounced wet and dry seasons.

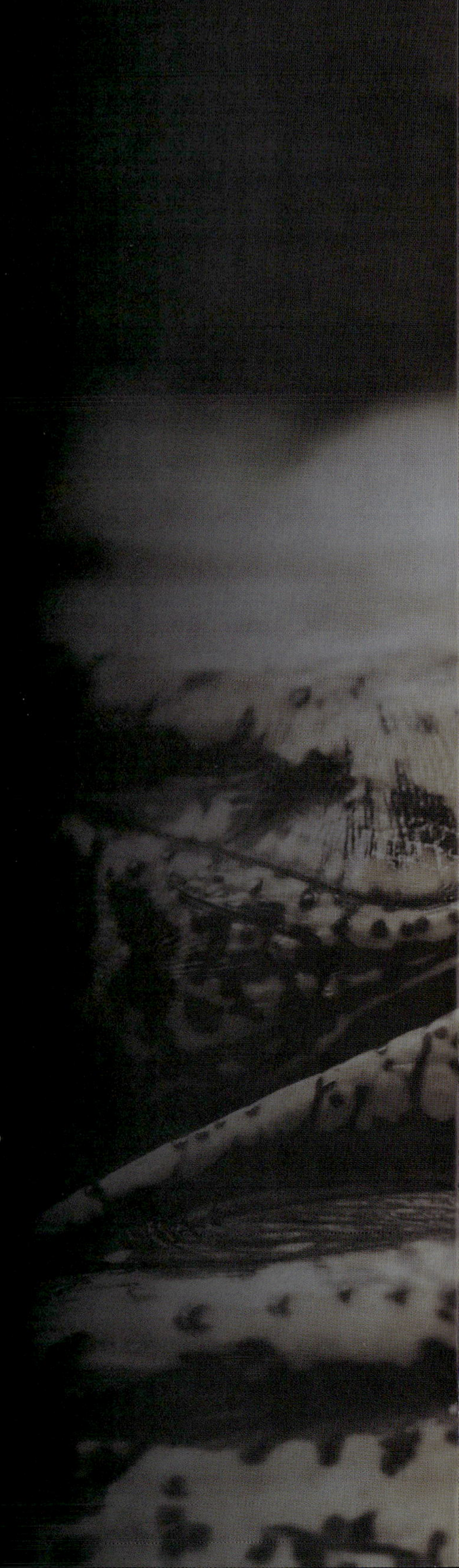